VOLUME 17

Contents

Heather Fenton is the new Editor of *Quiet Spaces*.

The Editor writes...

Welcome to this issue of *Quiet Spaces*. Our theme is 'Today' and I start us off by looking at a day in the life of Jesus. On this day, spending time with his disciples and many other people, how does he respond to what is happening around him, which includes the bad news about a family member, a crisis with a crowd, a teaching opportunity for the disciples and a stormy night?

Gordon Giles points out that it is very easy to think of today as simply the day between yesterday and tomorrow, but that, 'in music, for example, different things can happen all at once and for different durations of time, and yet we can inhabit the same space—and time—as all of them'. He uses Tavener's music to explore this, as it is 'not goal-orientated, rather it is music for the moment, where that moment is eternal'.

Running a retreat house is an all-consuming task, as I know from my own experience. There are endless calls on one's time for doing all sorts of things, and very little opportunity for 'being'. The door is never really shut. Finding personal space can be a real problem. Tim Blewett, the Warden of Launde Abbey, knows this too. He has written an article for us entitled 'Finding my own sanctuary'. You may not be involved in retreat house work, but each one of us, whatever our calling, needs this inner space. Drawing on his experience of living in Wales, Iraq and now at Launde Abbey, Tim shows something of his own struggle to do this because

Quiet Spaces

The brf prayer and spirituality journal

Today

Edited by Heather Fenton

Published by
The Bible Reading Fellowship
15 The Chambers, Vineyard
Abingdon, OX14 3FE
United Kingdom
Tel: +44 (0)1865 319700
Email: enquiries@brf.org.uk
Website: www.brf.org.uk
BRF is a Registered Charity

ISBN 978 1 84101 660 3
First published 2010
10 9 8 7 6 5 4 3 2 1 0

Acknowledgments
Scripture quotations taken from The Holy Bible, New International Version, copyright © 1973, 1978, 1984 by International Bible Society, are used by permission of Hodder & Stoughton, a member of the Hachette Livre UK Group. All rights reserved. 'NIV' is a registered trademark of International Bible Society. UK trademark number 1448790.

Scripture quotations taken from The Holy Bible, Today's New International Version. Copyright © 2004 by International Bible Society. Used by permission of Hodder & Stoughton, a member of the Hachette Livre UK Group. All rights reserved. 'TNIV' is a registered trademark of International Bible Society.

Scripture quotations taken from The New Revised Standard Version of the Bible, Anglicised Edition, copyright © 1989, 1995 by the Division of Christian Education of the National Council of the Churches of Christ in the USA, and are used by permission. All rights reserved.

Extracts from the Authorised Version of the Bible (The King James Bible), the rights in which are vested in the Crown, are reproduced by permission of the Crown's patentee, Cambridge University Press.

Scripture quotations taken from the Contemporary English Version of the Bible, published by HarperCollins Publishers, are copyright © 1991, 1992, 1995 American Bible Society.

A catalogue record for this book is available from the British Library

Printed by Harcourt Litho

although he is living in a 'place of stillness and tranquillity, it is certainly a struggle to draw closer to God'.

By the time you read this the winter will be in the past or in the future—not in your today, as it is in mine as I write. All that snow will seem like a strange dream as we sit in the garden enjoying the sun, the flowers and the birdsong. (Perhaps I am overoptimistic here. You will think so if the nearest you get to the garden today is sitting at the window watching the rain battering down again!) Anyway, Ann Persson has written a contribution entitled 'In the garden'. Ann often leads Quiet Days for BRF, and when I first heard of her she had just led one in a garden—so what better theme for a summer issue on which to ask her to write for us. Ann helps us to think about the possibilities of a quiet space in the garden at more or less any time of the year. We can use a garden as our focus, whether it is a garden that is large or small, in bloom or just with the potential for growth. Today may be a good time to sit and contemplate or go for a silent walk around the garden with God—'who saw all that he had made, and it was very good' (Genesis 1:31, NIV).

Naomi Starkey has written briefly about 'Living today and not the day after tomorrow'. Naomi starts off with a rather delightful story, which ends with the punch line: 'We travelled too fast yesterday and now we must wait for our souls to catch up with our bodies.' If you want to know more, read the article!

Carol, a Reader from rural Wales, has contributed some prayers; Margaret and Tony have their columns. Then there is some material from the BRF website www.barnabasinchurches.org.uk included in *Quiet Spaces* with the intention of encouraging you to see what other resources are available online. Finally, because we should not ignore previous 'todays', relegating them to a lost 'olden days', there are some things from the 'past'. Their contributions may be from a time well past but they have validity for us because their writers sought to see Christ in their today. May you find him in your today too!

article

HEATHER FENTON

A day in the life of Jesus

> ...a life where what happens next is **unknown**

We often hear the Gospels read, or study them ourselves, in bite-sized pieces. This way the stories and events tend to become more like self-contained episodes, appearing disconnected from one another. We give them names like 'the healing of the man born blind', 'the parable of the good Samaritan' or 'the Sermon on the Mount'. We lift them out of time so they become like an episode in an ongoing drama. If we think about our own experience, we realise that life is not like that. Even memorable events, like weddings, births and deaths, joys and disasters, have a 'before' and an 'after'.

This was so for Jesus and the people around him. They couldn't say, 'This is the word of the Lord,' and then sit down and get on with the next item on the worship agenda. They had to live in the context; they had to live with the consequences. It is good to remember that these are snapshots of part of real, lived life—a life where what happens next is unknown. We have the outline of the whole story

author

Heather Fenton works as a parish priest and editor of *The Reader* magazine.

of Jesus' life, so we know how it all turns out. The participants did not know what would happen next, even if there were some clues, which were largely missed as far as the disciples were concerned!

In Matthew 14 the author has grouped together a number of events in the same 24 hours, as if to remind us that this is what it could be like. If I were telling the children in school about these stories, I may well call them 'A day in the life of Jesus'—hence the title of this article.

Matthew 14 is a good chapter to use on a Quiet Day. It could be used at various parts of the day, or could form the basis of a longer retreat. It could also be used on a day which is not labelled anything special and may be all the better for that. If you want to take this last option, try reading the whole chapter at the beginning of a day. Then bring to mind the different events as they resonate with your day, while reading the newspaper, catching the news online or on television.

Jesus' day had begun badly. Many of us will have been there. A phone call, a text message, and everything changes. The plans for the day seem no longer appropriate. The news Jesus receives is horrific—a weak ruler, a sleazy party, a manipulative wife and a young girl being given a bleeding head on a plate. (No wonder the story has fascinated writers, artists and musicians throughout the ages.) For Jesus and his friends there is no doubt grief and maybe even fear. They live in politically unstable times when such things could happen to a friend. Jesus is part of the grieving and shocked extended family. Jesus' disciples bring him this news and so would have wanted to stick with him for the rest of his day.

Jesus' day had begun badly. Many of us will have been there. A phone call, a text message, and everything changes...

What comes to mind as you read this? Are there events in today's news that bring grief or fear? Is there something in your experience that has caused these responses? Spend a few moments praying for those involved. Ask for, or give thanks for, healing and courage.

The day continues to be different from what was expected. Jesus takes himself and his friends off in a boat to find a nice quiet place where they can grieve, talk, listen and pray together. But this sensible move is undermined. People are waiting. Maybe the news of John's beheading has spread and with it has come unease. John had been acclaimed as a prophet. Why did God allow this to happen to him?

Heedless of this, and not knowing or possibly not caring about Jesus' personal position, the crowds turn up anyway. The text simply says that Jesus had pity on them and healed their sick. You can almost hear the sigh as he resigns himself to getting on with it! Then he realises that they are hungry.

The disciples have not got a clue about what to do in such a situation, but Jesus tells them that sending the people away is just not an option! What else we can do? 'Is there a "Plan B"?' the disciples ask. Plan B turns out to be very unexpected, so much so that they would never have thought of it for themselves. It seems to me that what we expect God may do, and what he actually does, are usually two different things, and we would never have thought of his plan! But then, as it says, 'My thoughts are not your thoughts, neither are your ways my ways' (Isaiah 55:8, NIV).

If you are reading the chapter throughout the day, you could use the next bit while having lunch. Think about the supper-time events of the story. You could get into the story by imagining you were there. Why didn't you bring some food with you? Perhaps you were taken by surprise at hearing that Jesus was coming and just dashed off without thinking about it? Or were you too poor to have any supper? Did he speak for longer than you expected? What was your response to what happened about the provision of this food? Did you even notice how you came to have it? What would you have said to Jesus about it all if you had had the opportunity? You could imagine yourself being there, maybe as one of the crowd, a disciple or even the little boy. If you are a grandparent, would you have bored your grandchild many years later by telling the tale any number of times? 'Did I tell you of the day when...?' And there must have been many there that day who remembered it not for the free supper, but as 'the day when Auntie Hannah was healed', or 'the day when I met Jesus'.

Imaginative contemplation, this way of getting into a Bible passage, can be used for all sorts of stories. I love these spaces when you can sort of walk around in the Gospels.

I love these spaces when you can sort of walk around in the Gospels

The disciples would have remembered the feeding of the crowds above all, of course. So much for so many! The miracle happened in their hands. How would they not remember! Maybe this is why the story is told in various forms in all four Gospels. It was obviously something really important to the early Church. The task had seemed impossible. They had laughably few resources (how familiar does that sound?), only what they had received from Jesus—and there was food for all!

We can see specific instances when Jesus is seen to be in charge of a particular part of his creation

Faced with the task of telling the world about Jesus, they must have come back to this story again and again.

A busy life and circumstances over which we have no control can eat away at our 'quality time' with God and the quiet spaces that we need. I love the way Jesus is really determined to find some space, even if it comes at the end of a very full day. So he finishes sorting things out, says goodbye to people, sees the disciples safely on their way and then goes up the hill to pray. If you are meditating on Matthews 14 over a day, are you going to have time to reflect on the day and to look back with God over all that has gone on?

Maybe Jesus agonised over what had happened to John. Maybe he thought about his relatives, who were also grieving for John. I expect he talked to the Father about the events of the day and the people he had met. Maybe he prayed for some things and people—friends, family and faces from the crowd. Or maybe he just sat with his Father, too tired to turn it all into words. Maybe he even fell asleep. Who knows? If you are reading this chapter on retreat, perhaps you could simply sit with God for a time. If you are still in the middle of a working day, perhaps you could pause for a few minutes or pop into a church or sit in a park.

Jesus, alone and refreshed, sees his friends battling with a head wind on the Sea of Galilee. He just goes to help them. Walking on water seems very out of character, so I wonder if he was so full of the day's events, and having just spent time with his Father, and really loving his friends, he did it without thinking. He simply forgot that, in the wilderness after his baptism, he had decided not to make this sort of 'drawing attention to oneself' gesture. Perhaps he remembered his decision only when it was too late to go back.

Whatever was going on, it is a wonderfully reassuring story. For us who live in the 21st century and are continuously told of the threat we face from tidal flows, storms, high winds and all the other symptoms of global warming, it is surely a story for our times. Christ, 'through whom all things were made' (John 1:3) is seen to be able to walk where no man has walked before—on water! If we put this together with the other lake incident in which Jesus stills the storm (Mark 4:35–41), we can see specific instances when Jesus is seen to be in charge of a particular part of his creation. That which is general is also specific to a particular situation. You could pause at this point and think what it means to know that Jesus is Lord of all creation. What will this mean for you, for your children and your grandchildren? Is the return of Jesus, which we anticipate with joy each Advent, to be a reality in our life time? And will that coming be in some way associated with what is happening to creation if things become as bad as some people anticipate they might?

> A busy life and circumstances over which we have no control can eat away at our 'quality time' with God

More traditionally, this story has often been viewed as a wonderfully reassuring story for times when faith wavers. Generations of Christians have been grateful for the gloriously vulnerable Peter, who is willing to try anything and then discovers that walking on water means you get wet and rather seasick!

I thought for a long time that Jesus' response to Peter was one of rebuke or at best exasperation. After all, it was only hours since the disciples had seen five loaves and two fish being made into enough for a vast crowd! But now he speaks with a loving chuckle as he reaches out to grab Peter by the hair before he goes under. Jesus, the Word who became flesh (John 1:14), also speaks words of reassurance. 'Take courage! It is I. Don't be afraid' (Matthew 14:27). The phrase 'it is I' comes in the middle of this short quotation. The 'I'

Do you fear what tomorrow will hold? God knows.

He will be there

So the day is over…

who is at the middle is the 'I' who is in the middle. The One through whom all things were made now speaks.

The Bible is so full of exhortations not to be afraid, reminding us of our tendency to be afraid. Losing one's nerve is part of the human condition, and God understands this. The disciples have had a very big day. They worship him in amazement, saying, 'Truly you are the Son of God' (v. 33b). Jesus accepts their praise.

So the day is over. Or is it? By the time we get to this point, they are nearing land and daylight has come again. People are recognising Jesus. They are bringing their sick. The word is being sent, in true country fashion, all round the community. 'Come now! Jesus is here!' And how can Jesus resist? Another day has begun for him and his disciples.

We do not know all about what this day holds. As John says at the end of his Gospel, 'Jesus did many other things as well. If every one of them were written down, I suppose that even the whole world would not have room for the books that would be written' (John 21:25). Such is every tomorrow until it has been lived, lived with Jesus, the Lord of all, the One who says of himself: 'I am the Alpha and the Omega, the First and the Last, the Beginning and the End' (Revelation 22:13).

So, are you tired now? What have you discovered today? Do you fear what tomorrow will hold? God knows. He will be there. Therefore, 'don't be afraid' (Matthew 14:27). And it reminds me of the day I discovered that little phrase, when I was only a very young, inexperienced Christian full of problems and fears: 'Fear not, little flock; for it is your Father's good pleasure to give you the kingdom' (Luke 12:32, KJV). Some of my personal tomorrows, which of course have since become yesterdays, tell me that that is true.

GORDON GILES

Music for today's soul

One of the criminals who were hanged there kept deriding him and saying, 'Are you not the Messiah? Save yourself and us!' But the other rebuked him, saying, 'Do you not fear God, since you are under the same sentence of condemnation? And we indeed have been condemned justly, for we are getting what we deserve for our deeds, but this man has done nothing wrong.' Then he said, 'Jesus, remember me when you come into your kingdom.' He replied, 'Truly I tell you, today you will be with me in Paradise.'

LUKE 23:39–43 (NRSV)

author

Gordon Giles is Vicar of St Mary Magdalene, Enfield and Director of Post-ordination Training for the Edmonton Area of the Diocese of London. He has written several books, including *Fasting and Feasting* (BRF, 2008).

We all live in various time zones. We can consult a clock, and be assured of the time in whichever part of the world we are standing, but if it is midday in London, it is 1 p.m. in Paris, 6 a.m. in Toronto and 8 p.m. in Beijing. Lunchtime in England is breakfast time on US America's East Coast and supper time in China. Strange as this is, we hardly question it: time zones are a fact of modern, international life, and in the last century we have got used to them. 'Today' is sometimes already 'tomorrow' in another part of the world, and at the same time 'yesterday' may barely have finished elsewhere.

In 1884 Standard Time was introduced to eliminate the problems caused by the use of solar time in each place (Bristol, for example, was ten minutes behind London). Invented in the late 1870s by the Canadian railway planner Sir Sandford Fleming, Standard Time involves 24 standard meridians of longitude (north–south lines, 15° apart), with Greenwich being the prime meridian. Consequently, our modern notion of 'today' is fundamentally different from the todays of yesterday! According to the dictates of Standard Time, 'today' began on the Pacific Island of Kiritimati, and it is there that the New Year is celebrated first. John Ellerton (1826–93), writing only 14 years before Standard Time was introduced formally, wrote a missionary hymn which contains these evocative lines:

As o'er each continent and island
The dawn leads on another day,
The voice of prayer is never silent,
Nor dies the strain of praise away.

The sun that bids us rest is waking
Our brethren 'neath the western sky,
And hour by hour fresh lips are making
Thy wondrous doings heard on high.

Reflecting a thoroughly modern concept of 'today', the hymn reminds us that, while different places are celebrating different times of day, we are basically all human, doing the same kinds of things, and that all sorts of activities are

While different places are celebrating different times of day, we are basically all human, doing the same kinds of things...

taking place simultaneously. Thus the notion of 'now' is still distinct from clock time. 'Now' is 'now' in France, Sydney and New York, even if it is not 'today' at the same time. Telephones and emails bring this home to us.

Our predecessors, who had no electric light, had a different approach. Although Ancient Egyptian days began at sunrise, the Jewish practice which was carried into medieval Europe was to begin the day at sunset. The idea of a day running from midnight to midnight is a modern convention. It is very easy to think of today as simply the day between yesterday and tomorrow. In this way we see life as linear, that is, moving from one point to another, lengthening the past and shortening the future. Life is one thing after another, and this is how we assume human time works. This approach can be quite depressing or confusing, and St Augustine thought so too. He reckoned that if the past had already finished and the future not yet started, there was literally no time for 'now'. There was, as he put it, no space between the past and the future. However, linear time is not the only kind of time.

In music, for example, different things can happen all at once and for different durations of time, and yet we can inhabit the same space—and time—as all of them. Musical time works on different levels, sometimes all at once. Melody and harmony and rhythm combine time zones that flow simultaneously in a world we have no difficulty entering. Musical time reminds us that there is more than one way of looking at and experiencing time.

> It is very easy to think of today as simply the day between yesterday and tomorrow

While it is true that each of us lives in a particular time zone (such as London), we also live and move about within other time zones. Our 'todays' are not simply periods of 24 hours beginning at midnight, during which lots of individual, distinct, measurable events take place. We might well ask of someone, 'What did you do today?', but all kinds of other things can happen to us other than what we 'did' today.

We have different *experiences* of time passing. Today we might eat a meal, drive a car, listen to music, take a nap, attend a boring meeting and speak for five minutes to a good friend. Time will 'pass' differently in each of these cases. And we might even attend an act of worship. As a vicar, I conduct weddings and funerals. A funeral lasts 25 minutes in a crematorium. A wedding lasts 50 minutes in church. But a wedding is shorter than a funeral. What I mean, of course, is that it 'feels' shorter, and that is important. It is a more profound manifestation of the old adage, 'time flies when you're having fun'. It is nonsense, but true. Similarly, while I am having fun with my friends (when time passes quickly), you might be doing the housework (which will take an age!), yet we may well have both spent the very same hour doing both.

> God's time is different too. It probably isn't linear...

God's time is different too. It probably isn't linear: it doesn't have a beginning, a middle and an end, like a novel. This is difficult to grasp when we are locked into a humanly conceptualised linear time continuum. But such a way of understanding time cannot command our loyalty in any, or every, event. We each live in multiple time zones, and also in our own unique time zone. And the most important and the most useful one is God's time zone. God's time, unlike ours, is not transient, fleeting and finite.

God's time is not easy to grasp, but in baptism we may have a clue. Baptism doesn't make any sense outside God's time, but only in the context of eternity. In baptism we are washed and welcomed into the life of the Holy Spirit, and this means that our lives are not simply going to be one event after another until there is no time for any more and all is washed away by the great tide of time like a castle built with sand. Rather we are held by God in the tide of eternity: the tide that comes and goes but never ends. In baptism we are welcomed by God's Holy Spirit into an eternal time zone of love and hope and freedom.

The English contemporary composer John Tavener has attempted to express the idea of God's time in his music. You may be familiar with his cello work, *The Protecting Veil*, or his brief choral piece, *The Lamb*, which is often sung at Christmas Carol services. In 1977 Tavener converted to Russian Orthodoxy, and in his music we find simplicity, characterised by the use of Byzantine and Russian chant, and an attempt to evoke great spaces and a certain sense of timelessness. His music does not 'go' anywhere. It is often immensely slow, sometimes with long periods of silence. This is because Tavener believes that complexity can be a manifestation of evil (thus that simplicity can reflect goodness and the divine). He also sees composition as penitential. His music has been described by himself and others as 'iconic', implying that his works can somehow transmit eternity to hearers. Icons were instrumental in Tavener's conversion, and he considers them to be the pinnacle of Christian art. Much of his music overtly stresses the metaphorical idea that he is doing with music what iconographers do with visual images: opening up an eternal world of the divine to sight or sound. In his *We Shall See Him as He Is* (1990), eleven of the 13 movements are titled 'Ikon'. Tavener also employs the extended drone (*ison*), which acts as a harmonic thread, representing and connecting us to the eternal.

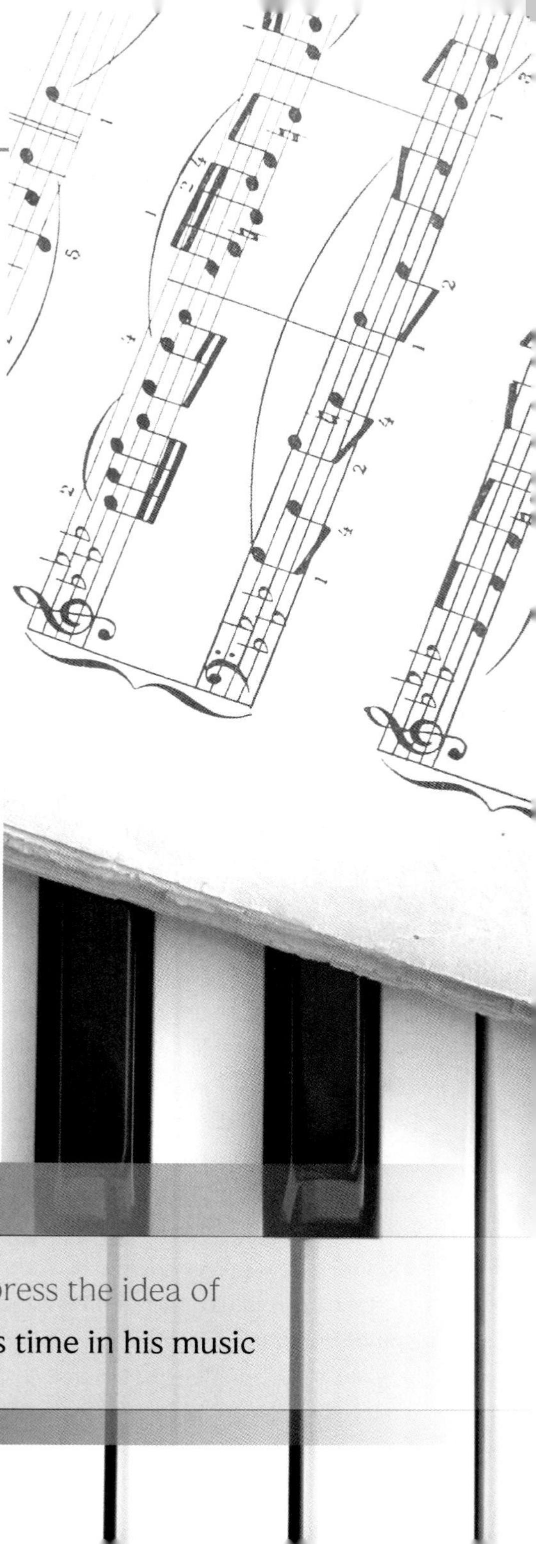

…express the idea of

God's time in his music

© Sur / IStock.com

Tavener's music is not goal-orientated; rather, it is music for the moment, where that moment is eternal. There is little argument, conflict or resolution of established tensions, and a corresponding rejection of any psychologically significant dimension to his music (such as angst, guilt or grief). A lack of change or motion makes his music seem static. Such timelessness locates us in eternity, but also in the present moment, which therefore become linked, both inside and outside of time. By the same token, Tavener's works are not characterised by strong beginnings and endings but often involve silence, as though we have turned up and down the volume on something that was already happening, and continues to do so after the work has 'ended'. What we hear today is a continuation of what we would have heard yesterday and which continues tomorrow. Like Christ, perhaps, it is 'the same yesterday and today and forever' (Hebrews 13:8).

Such timelessness locates us in eternity, but also in the present moment

Of course, music has duration and cannot be timeless in itself. We cannot actually stop completely still, and just as there is no such thing as absolute silence, timelessness is unachievable too. Yet Tavener's attempt to express the ineffable and transport listeners out of this world to a time and place inhabited by God is appealing, and many (not all of whom are practising Christians) see value in Tavener's non-directional, static music. Some have described his music as arousing a state not unrelated to that engendered by drugs: a sense of an 'eternal now': of the present unwrapped and rolled out. Nevertheless, Tavener's avoidance of musical direction, change or motion is explicitly theological, and his intention is to express and illustrate eternal truths and divine presence and essence in musical terms. In a postmodern cultural context driven by and infected by multiplicity, in which temporal disorientation is ubiquitous, Tavener provides an undifferentiated, stable location. We are not good at relating to time (or the lack of it), and he provides an alternative to and distraction from the alienating hustle and bustle of modern life. Tavener invites us into a distinctively divine sound world where we may retreat into prayer and peace.

Tavener's concept of eternity as an extraterrestrial location, inhabited by God, overlooks the engagement and interaction that God has made with the world in Jesus Christ, whose incarnation is an event in time, through which God owns, occupies and redeems our time. Tavener downplays both the humanity of Christ, with its accompanying emotional struggles and difficulties, and the central focus of faith upon the passion of Jesus. Eternal life comes through resurrection, which itself is dependent on the real saving power of the cross.

Salvation is not just for eternity, but for now. Jesus tells the thief on the adjacent cross, 'today you will be with me in Paradise' (Luke 23:43), linking the here and now of today with the future hope of salvation and the past promise of redemption that we find in the Old Testament. The 'today' of the crucifixion is *the* day, the today that makes all future todays meaningful and hopeful. But that today is the intersection between God's time and ours—on *that* day, our today and God's united. And so they shall be again in the new creation. There is a sense of the 'now and not yet' to this comment of Christ's, for while God's time breaks in at that point, we are still awaiting, in our many todays, the final day, the last today, on which all shall be swept up in the glorious redemption of the children of God at Christ's return. So when Jesus says, 'today' you will be with me, he means, 'today, and later and forever'. And that is *the* time zone for which we were created.

Eternal life comes through resurrection, which itself is dependent on the real saving power of the cross

...we are still awaiting

TIM BLEWETT

Finding my own sanctuary

author

Prior to being Warden of Launde Abbey Retreat House in Leicestershire, Tim Blewett was Canon Residentiary of St Asaph Cathedral. Between these two posts he has served as Army Chaplain in Iraq to the HQ National Support Element and the Baghdad Support Unit. He currently leads retreats, acts as a spiritual director to many and preaches and teaches across the country.

Perhaps I shouldn't admit this as the warden of a retreat house: I wonder sometimes whether God is there as I struggle with my prayer life and in the reading of scripture. Prayer is often difficult and as I read scripture I strive for greater understanding and clarity. However much I struggle, though, it is important to persevere.

Last year was particularly busy at Launde Abbey. We created a hermitage (for our guests who are looking for greater silence) and also established camping facilities for the many who want to camp, especially young people. The park and ha-ha to the front of the Abbey were also restored. Just after Easter 2009 we launched a public campaign to raise £1million to save Launde Abbey as a retreat house. At the time of writing, we are nearly there and I hope we will have achieved our goal by the end of 2009. The huge generosity of so many people—with the vast majority of gifts coming from ordinary people who use the Abbey—says a lot about how special a place Launde Abbey is. It has enabled us to start work on this project, in which a total of £2.6million will be spent on redeveloping the Main Tudor-Elizabethan House. It is due to be completed at the end of November 2010. Launde Abbey has gone from strength to strength and we have won yet another award from East Midlands Tourism—three in three years. Numbers of those using Launde Abbey have increased. Those coming to Launde Abbey range from individuals coming on retreat to the piloting of retreats for primary school children. Retreat should be seen as being open to all.

But where is God in all that busyness? Is it possible to draw closer to the divine while doing so much in a church which seems to value only activity? Often we get confused, thinking that we come to him, whereas God comes to us. We think that if only we do this or that we are advancing the kingdom of God and drawing closer to him. God, however, is beyond our reach, but he can come to us. We are not beneath his love, his mercy, his forgiveness, his charity. We can glimpse him in those around us, in his word, invisibly in our souls, and more visibly in the Eucharist or Communion. We need to have eyes to see and ears to hear so that we can start to discern God's presence.

Is it possible to draw closer to the divine while doing so much in a church which seems to value only activity?

We need to go back to the basics of the Christian journey and start afresh. In our 'doing' we are often expressing something of our own needs and little or nothing of God. We do not discern God's calling but rather get it confused with our own desires and thoughts. I can remember when I was in training to be a priest, a cleric, to whom I had been sent on placement, taught me an important lesson. He said that I should visit someone who was the spiritual

Launde Abbey
has gone from strength to strength

> She had an inner strength

powerhouse of that particular parish. When I knocked on the door of their house, I expected to be greeted by a dynamic individual but instead was met by someone who had struggled to get to the door. The lady was all but housebound but as she prayed through lists sent to her by the parish priest, she had become the spiritual powerhouse of the parish. She had an inner strength of love that radiated from her in a way that I had not witnessed before. She was steeped in prayer and in the scriptures. It is in our prayer and in our reading of the Bible that we open ourselves up to God, calling him in as we draw him out of those around us as they draw him out in us. Retreat houses provide space for people to do this—listening discerningly to God's call through grappling with prayer and scripture.

In my ministry, whether in Wales, Iraq or at Launde Abbey, I have continuously come across people who are searching, often looking beyond themselves and missing the fact that God is with them already. We do not have to become worthier to find union with God or to do something by our own efforts to pull ourselves up into heaven. Whatever we do, we will never be worthy of God, but we are bound to him as we are made in his image.

As we try to pull ourselves up in to heaven we are actually putting ourselves in the place of God. We think we can do it on our terms, in our own way. Instead we need to learn, through our life of prayer, that we need to empty ourselves of our own hubris—of our very self—and allow God to be at our centre. It is only in emptying ourselves and putting our priorities to one side that we can possibly attain unity in God.

How do we do that? Firstly, we need to empty ourselves so that God can be at our centre. God must be at the heart of our vocation. This is sometimes a struggle for those who are actively engaged on a spiritual journey. In the busyness of Launde Abbey for me as warden, despite it being a place of stillness and tranquillity, it is certainly a struggle to draw closer to God. Secondly, the discipline of prayer is central to my struggle. The saying of the daily round of Morning, Evening and Night Prayer and that of the Eucharist provides the wallpaper or background of prayer, allowing the Bible to be read in an organised way while maintaining an ongoing prayer life that includes the concerns of the Church, the world and Launde Abbey. It is in this prayer, and through individual personal devotion, and through the reading of scripture, that it is possible to glimpse the divine reality of God. Thirdly, it is also important to have someone who is that little bit further ahead in the spiritual journey to act as our guide. So, it is in emptying ourselves and putting God at our centre, in prayer and in reading scripture and by having a spiritual guide that we can move forward in our spiritual journey.

> ...it is certainly a struggle to draw closer to God

When we stop and look for the divine, we realise that God is with us.

> More and more demands are crowding in on our time—from family and friends, from work and our social life and, dare I say it, even from the church

In that moment our faith is re-excited and we can see clearly. But it is difficult for many of us to stop and refocus for three reasons. Firstly, we are caught up in the frenetic pace of life. More and more demands are crowding in on our time—from family and friends, from work and our social life and, dare I say it, even from the church. Secondly, we can become so overwhelmed by life that even when we try to stop, our minds are still racing, full of distractions that crowd in on us. Thirdly, because of that feverish pace of life we are often worn out and suffer from anxieties or even depression, and we do not allow our soul to find any rest. Going on retreat is therefore important. It gives us space to find stillness, tranquillity and a sanctuary in which we can find safety and wholeness in God. It is in the learning to put to one side all that society—and we—so often value that we find out the true values in life as we glimpse the divine.

As we change our values, we find that we can be busy by the standards of the world, but at our centre is a stillness and a strength that comes from God. We then grow in confidence in our spiritual journey as we mature in God's love. We start to develop a oneness with God—but it is a long journey and we constantly have to come back to prayer and scripture, emptying ourselves of ourselves. In doing so, we gain clarity through prayer and scripture as we no longer procrastinate, flipping from one thing to another. Our whole body, mind and soul yearn for God as we learn to love God and our neighbour as we love ourselves. We are enabled to make a gear change which, through the love of God, propels us forward in the spiritual journey.

In this moment we stop judging others as we no longer judge ourselves, knowing that the love of God calls us forward in our calling. We know, just as Peter knew when he denied Christ three times before the cock crowed twice (see Matthew 26:75) , that we are committed to Christ. God lives in us, forgiving us, and even though we are not worthy of Christ, we are bound to him. This depth of intimacy in God is perplexing, frightening and incomprehensible all at the same time. In that moment, which may only be fleeting, we embrace God with our meagre love, knowing that God gives himself for us in selfless love. In that moment, we also learn that we cannot hold on to or possess what we have been given, however much we perhaps try. God gives without measure in his abundance while we turn him into our victim.

God is so much more than just being the victim, as his relationship with us shows. He sees in us things that we cannot see. He recognises that we are people with talents and gifts, if only we could be set free to use them. If we could only recognise what we have been made, we would then fulfil our vocation, doing those things that only we can do and becoming the people we are called to be. Christ's desire is to present us along with himself to God, lifting us high and by his grace taking us into the heart of God. We know that our hunger and thirst will be satisfied by God in this moment, however transitory it is. It is in this hope that we are transformed and the resurrection of Christ becomes a reality as we enter into his peace.

As we put to one side our hubris we recognise that nothing can be compared to God. It is meaningless to try to compare anything to him. Yet we are still tempted to compare so much with God, even though it is facile and pointless. It is a lesson that we need to relearn continually: getting our priorities right so that God is at our centre and that if we need anything then all we are to do is to 'ask and you will receive' (John 16:24, NIV). It is in that moment that I find my sanctuary.

God is so much more than just being the victim, as his relationship with us shows

ANN PERSSON

In the garden

> ...a sense of
> new beginnings

It was a warm morning in June and it had rained during the night, so the air was moist and perfumed. It was heady in the rose garden and pungent among the herbs. I noticed the designer of the gardens also wandering along the grass paths enjoying the scented air. She knew that it would be a magical experience and I shared it with her. It is a memory that has remained with me.

Gardens are evocative spaces. In the garden of our former home was a stand of white foxgloves, one of my favourite plants. One night, there was a full moon, and everywhere was bathed in silver light. I had the impulse to go outside and walk in the garden. When I came across the foxgloves, they seemed to glow like lit candles—a wonderful sight!

Britain is a country of gardens, all shapes and sizes and most of them urban. The owners have designed, fashioned and nurtured parcels of land to create landscapes, be it on a small or a grand scale. The word 'garden' has the same origin as the German *Garten*, which are both related to the word 'enclosure'. In the Middle East, gardens are private and secluded, usually surrounded by a wall. In this country, too, they are, for the most part, bounded by hedges, walls or

author

Ann Persson enjoys combining her love of nature and her love of God's word. She leads Quiet Days and her first book, *The Circle of Love*, was published by BRF in 2010.

fences. So to sit in a garden has a sense of containment and therefore restfulness—if you can keep your eyes from looking at the work that needs to be done!

Gardens are significant places in the Bible. Recently, I led a Quiet Day for BRF, using a garden as the base for a reflection on four gardens mentioned in the Bible. We stood by a beautiful herbaceous border to read the passage in Genesis that describes Eden, the garden that God had planted in the east and where he put the man that he had formed (Genesis 1:9–13). It was the garden of God's original intention for humanity, created to reflect God's glory and for the enjoyment of the entire created order. He intended that we should live in harmonious relationship with him and with everything that he had made, but the man and the woman he had created chose to go their own way. They abused the gift of life, followed their own plans, and the harmony of the garden was shattered and this resulted in exclusion.

It was the garden of God's original intention for humanity

Beyond the herbaceous border was a black door that led to the working area—the greenhouse and potting sheds, and so on. As we read about God's decision to drive out Adam and Eve from the garden of Eden, so we walked through the door and shut it behind us. It was very impacting to stand on the other side and feel excluded from all that God had intended for us. Paradise (the word is of Persian origin and also means 'garden') became paradise lost, and Adam and Eve became wanderers on the face of the earth. Humanity needed some sort of rescue plan.

The impact of the tragedy of the broken relationships that thread their way through the Old Testament leads us to another garden, the Garden of Gethsemane or the Garden of the Oil Press. For our next reflection, we chose a small area that was shaded by a mulberry and a walnut tree and was hidden from view of the house. Gethsemane was an enclosed olive grove on the Mount of Olives that Jesus used to frequent with his disciples. Olive trees are ancient symbols of peace and reconciliation. We speak of 'offering the olive branch'. Olive oil was used for healing in the ancient Middle East so it is ironic, or fitting, that Jesus should pray here before being arrested. But it was not without struggle, and his time in the Garden of Gethsemane was a time of great anguish. Contemplating what it would mean nearly broke him apart and he cried out, 'Father, if you are willing, take this cup from me; yet not my will, but yours be done' (Luke 22:42, NIV). We used a recording of the final movement of Tchaikovsky's Sixth Symphony to help us to get in touch with a tiny fraction of the anguish that Jesus suffered. The following day, he faced the cruellest, most barbaric death—death by crucifixion. The death of Jesus, who is also described as the second Adam, made possible our peace and reconciliation with God and promises healing for our lives and ultimately for the nations.

We walked one by one and at intervals through a tunnel of rhododendrons, no longer in flower, sensing the long, dark wait that the disciples and the women endured on the sabbath as Jesus lay buried in the tomb. We emerged into the light and gathered on the path by a large pond to think about the extraordinary event which took place in a garden, as dawn broke over Jerusalem. The stone that had sealed the tomb, where the body of Jesus had been laid, was rolled back and

Gardens are significant places in the Bible

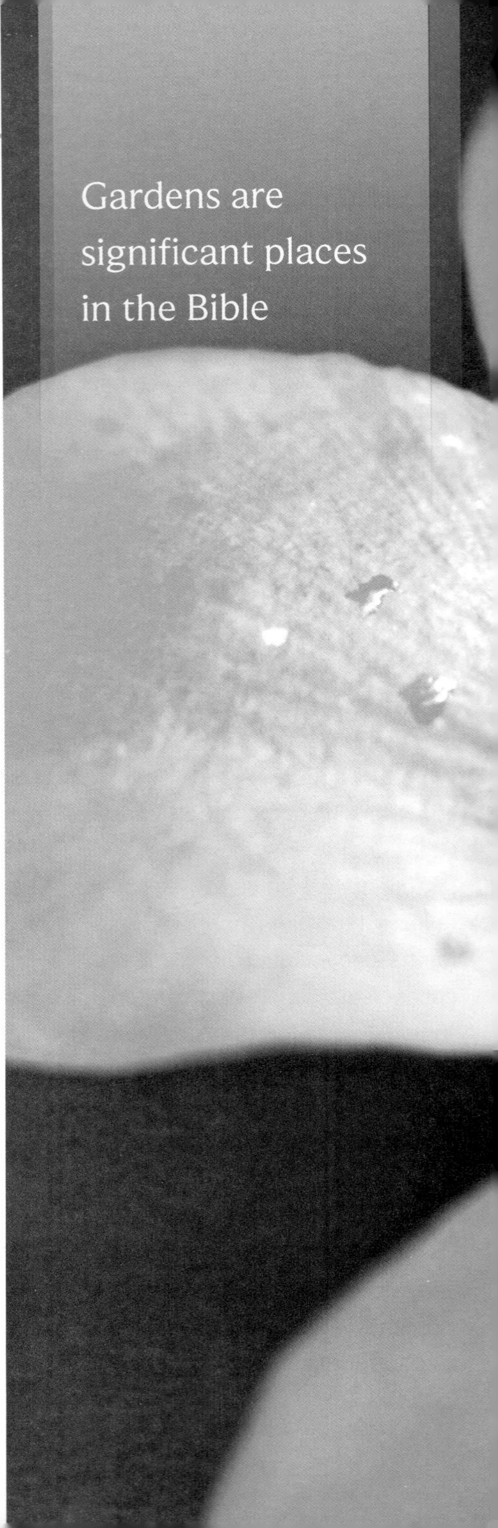

© Bonita R. Cheshier / Shutterstock.com

the tomb was empty, except for the grave clothes. Mary Magdalene had come with spices to embalm the body, and to her dismay she found that he had vanished. Then came that amazing moment when she heard her name being called and recognised the risen Jesus. He did not allow her to cling to him but instead he gave her a gospel to proclaim. We left the pond and walked through a stone arch to the area where the cars had been parked and there was the sound of passing traffic on the road. We, too, have a gospel to proclaim in our brief life time to the troubled world in which we live.

Gardens through the seasons of the year are rich resources for contemplation

God's amazing plan...

The last garden that is mentioned in scripture is in Revelation 22:1–6, where there is the river of the water of life that flows from the throne of God, down the middle of the city. On each side of the river stands the tree of life, bearing twelve crops of fruit, and the leaves are for the healing of the nations. No longer will there be any curse. It could be called paradise regained.

The gardens of the Bible tell a story of beauty and brokenness leading to healing and restoration through Jesus Christ, the Lamb of God.

We left feeling awed by God's amazing plan of salvation into which we were gathered. Finding a garden, maybe your own, and meditating on the biblical gardens is an exercise that you could repeat for yourself and for others.

Gardens through the seasons of the year are rich resources for contemplation, although the weather may not always be favourable for sitting too long! They are not only filled with the plants and other features that we have placed there but are visited by butterflies and a host of insects and birds that sing for us. The sky above forms a canopy that is always changing in colour and patterns, from a vast expanse of blue to grey streaks and stormy rain clouds; crimson-flushed sunsets and early morning mists; fluffy white cumulus clouds to star-spangled night skies. And there are the two great lights to illuminate the garden, the sun by day and the moon by night. Our little plot is filled with the wonder of God's creation.

Seasonal themes for meditation abound in gardens. The late summer and early autumn are periods of fruitfulness, the culmination of the botanical year, and this can lead to an exploration of the fruitfulness in our own lives. We had a young pear tree that was laden with fruit last year, so much so that the branches were bent low by the weight of the crop and in danger of breaking. It was a powerful image that made me stop and think about my own life and busyness. Do I need to prune back or remove some fruit to protect my tree?

There are seed heads bursting to disperse their seed. Nature uses many forms of dispersal, for example wind for dandelions, thistledown and sycamores; animals and birds as seed carriers, or force, as the sun dries the pods and they twist and eject their seeds. Violets, lupins and broom use this method. This reminds me that there are many ways of dispersing the seed of God's love, and I ask myself what ways I use to spread his gospel.

In the autumn nature is preparing for the challenges of winter. The garden is dressed in bright colours as the trees and shrubs are breaking down the chlorophyll and reabsorbing the sugar contained in their leaves. Eventually they will lose the leaves so that they can conserve the moisture that they will need in harsher conditions. Birds have put on their winter plumage and furry creatures have thicker coats. Butterflies and insects have found somewhere to hide, while squirrels are scampering around, amassing their store of nuts for the leaner period ahead, provided they can remember where they put them! Walking in the garden gives me the opportunity to reflect on how I cope with the hard conditions that occur in life from time to time. Do I toughen up and put on a thicker coat or feed off the memories of better times or, like the trees, batten down and simplify until

...an exploration of the fruitfulness in our own lives

spring comes? Maybe I catch a falling leaf and think about what it means to surrender and to let go in a particular situation that confronts me.

In winter, the skeleton branches of trees display their intricate form against the pale grey sky. Frost outlines the plants and edges the grass with silver. Thick fog gives an air of mystery and the lashing of wind and rain are images of strength and power. The hours of daylight are fewer and the temperatures have plummeted. The garden either sleeps or is battered but, underneath the ground, the bulbs are building up their stores of energy as they prepare for the thrust of spring. The idea I like to reflect on is that 'hope is the winter name of God'.

The lengthening of daylight hours and the increasing warmth from the sun are triggers for spring to erupt in glory. God displays his faithfulness in our gardens. Snowdrops are the first to appear; birds begin to sing again as they find their partners; there are tadpoles in the pond; blossom is abundant and a riot of daffodils have pushed their way through the softening earth. We, too, can feel a surge of energy and a sense of new beginnings that lead us to worship the God of creation, and where better to do it but in a garden.

Now it is summer; the flowers of spring are over. The vegetable seeds that we may have sown earlier are producing good things for us to eat and to share with others; hopefully, we are enjoying sunny days and the chance to get together with friends and family for meals in the garden, which is in bloom.

Summer is a good time to sit and contemplate or to go for a silent walk around the garden or a park with God, 'who saw all that he had made, and it was very good' (Genesis 1:31).

Ask him for eyes to see nature as if for the first time. Awaken your senses.

Take time to look, listen, touch and smell. Feel the nurturing earth beneath your feet and be aware of the sky above, the unseen planets and stars. Sense your special place in God's created order.

Sit quietly for a while and let your inner silence lead you into worship.

The kiss of the sun for pardon,
the song of the birds for mirth,
one is nearer God's heart in a garden
than anywhere else on earth.

So wrote Mrs Dorothy Frances Gurney (1858–1932). It is certainly a fact that gardens are places where God is revealed to us and he longs to meet us there—maybe today.

My Space

This space is for you to make your own notes.

St Brendan and his companions set out one day on a pilgrimage into the unknown. This sculpture can be seen at Cahersiveen on the Ring of Kerry.

NAOMI STARKEY

Living today and not the day after tomorrow

A story is told of an early 20th-century Western explorer who hired a team of men to carry his kit on a trek deep into the African rainforest. On the first day, the pace was brisk and they covered a good distance. On the second day, however, the porters refused to move but simply sat and rested. When the tetchy explorer asked their leader to explain, he replied, 'We travelled too fast yesterday and now we must wait for our souls to catch up with our bodies.'

This story has been used in sermons and books to make the point that life needs to be balanced; we should not live in such a whirl of activity that body and soul do not keep pace with one another. What if, however, our problem is the opposite one—that the dreams of our hearts and the possibilities we see in our circumstances continually outstrip our day-by-day reality? What if

author

Naomi Starkey is a commissioning editor at BRF and also editor of *New Daylight*. She has written *Good Enough Mother* (2009) and *Pilgrims to the Manger* (2010) for BRF.

we spend much of our time feeling that life is too short to allow events to move as slowly as they do? Rather than our feet moving faster than our souls, our souls are so far ahead that our feet are worn out trying to keep pace.

Impatience and frustration can easily become a bubble around us in which we live, move and breathe but never quite connect with those around us. They may be very happy with living 'today' while we are solely focused on 'tomorrow', if not 'the day after the day after that'. Our attitude is unlikely to be challenged by our late-modern consumer-driven society either. These days, it is easy to assume that pretty much anything is available in 'ready to use' format, from cook-chill food so good that it seems home-made to church plants that come with a pre-formed leadership team, healthy finances and fired-up congregation. The opportunities to learn patience and to value the slow unfolding of process are, more likely than not, to be limited.

Of course, the ability to see possibilities is a valuable one. A much-quoted verse in relation to church leadership is the one about 'where there is no vision, the people perish' (Proverbs 29:18, KJV). The trouble is that for some people the vision can be so overpowering that they are inclined to overlook the hard decisions (and concomitant consequences) necessary for the vision to be realised. It is as if an architect dreams of an awe-inspiring skyscraper but is then tempted to abandon the project in frustration during the two years it takes to clear the site, dig down and establish the foundations.

Impatience and frustration can easily become a bubble around us in which we live, move and breathe but never quite connect with those around us

Being the sort of person who focuses on what could be rather than what is (or even what is particularly likely) can also lead us to premature panic. A year ago, a member of my family started down the dark tunnel of doctors' appointments, hospital referrals, tests and more tests—and I was terrified, anticipating a verdict of mortal illness, a painful, long-drawn-out and untimely death. I cried, raged, swore at God… and had to repent when the final diagnosis was a relatively simple and manageable condition.

…the only way to get to tomorrow is via today, **hour by hour, step by step**

In the Sermon on the Mount, Jesus told his audience: 'Do not worry about tomorrow, for tomorrow will worry about itself. Each day has enough trouble of its own' (Matthew 6:34, TNIV). His words are both consolation for those who fear what the future might hold but also a challenge for those who chafe against the plodding pace of their present circumstances. To state the blindingly obvious: the only way to get to tomorrow is via today, hour by hour, step by step. While it can be energising to have a sense of where life is going, we should not be paralysed with boredom by the prospect of going through the necessary stages to reach our destination—a destination which, moreover, may turn out simply to be the next stage in the journey and not a finishing point at all.

As someone with a tendency to impatience and predisposition to enjoying most kinds of change, the idea of eternal life as shining, immutable bliss always struck me as—dare I admit it?—a touch tedious. As I have come to glimpse an infinitesimal bit of the unfathomable greatness of God, however, I have started to realise that 'heaven' does not necessarily mean that all our visions, hopes and longings are fulfilled there and then in the presence of the Father, with nothing left to happen after that. Instead, it occurs to me that perhaps every moment of eternity is imbued with significance and wonder as we learn to delight in an unending succession of 'todays', however hard we may have found this to do previously. Above all, God himself will show us, with infinite grace and delight, just how much more we can learn about what it means to love and to be loved by him.

Transforming encounter

You may want to use this with a small group, with one or two people leading.

Moses encounters God...

Introductory Prayers

Reader: We have come at the
invitation of our God,
called into this place
called into this time
called into the presence of God.
Reader: The God of Abraham
who taught humanity to gaze
to the stars
and await—
generation by generation—
the fulfilment of his promises.
Reader: The God of Isaac
conceived in the promise of angels—
delivered by the mercy of God
to bless his son as patriarch
founder of God's people.
Reader: The God of Jacob
who wrestled by night with his Creator
and at dawn received his blessing.
Reader: We come at the invitation of
our God—
the God whose call echoes across ages;
resounding in time and space
yet intimate—
entrancing...
Reader: A voice that calls us to
encounter:
to encounter with grace beyond
telling—
to encounter with healing and

transformation—
to encounter that calls us to stillness
and to awe—
to encounter with the presence whose
compassion brings healing—
the power that transforms
the love that cherishes us into
changing.

Music starts quietly under the introductory readings and then goes straight into

Song

'Be still, for the presence of the Lord'

Prayer

Lord God, you created a world of
beauty and majesty
entrusting it to the keeping of your
people.
Grace us with your presence
lead us to your truth
and bring us to perfection of faith,
hope and love.

Reading

Exodus 3:1–6, 9–12
Moses encounters God in the Burning Bush.

Reflection

It may be that the 'reflector' would prepare the meditation themselves, drawing from their own experience / spirituality.
This one is offered as a possibility—based on the idea of Moses reflecting on his encounter with God.

I *could* have walked by.
It was a strange sight to be sure…
but I could have walked past—
averted my eyes
and focused on the sheep.
(fondly) Silly animals!
But a full-time job…
A spouse—a family—a job…
I had no need to notice anything out of
the ordinary—
life was full—
life was good—
life was all I wanted it to be…
and yet
and yet I looked.
A bush—burning and yet not consumed
by the flame.
I was puzzled—

intrigued—
curious—
all that—
and yet more...
It was as if I was drawn—
I was called
I was pulled
I was invited...
It was not my initiative but that of...
(possible other voices—as if 'angels prompting'!)
that of something speaking to a
yearning I did not yet know I had—
that of something enfolding a desire so
deep it was hidden from me—
that of something—
of someone

History knows my name because God called it first

speaking in tones that resonated,
touched chords in me that vibrated with
the harmony of the heavens—
calling the deepest within
to the utterly beyond.
The bush was burning—
all that was needed of me was to notice—
to notice and not to walk by—
to notice and allow this thing I had
never seen before
to touch my curiosity—
to create an attraction that was easier
to act on than to ignore.
And once attracted...
ah, once attracted—
then I knew this was not about a
burning bush—
this was not an interruption to a day
going about my daily business—
not an aside.
God had stepped into the ordinariness
of a day
and enticed me to step into the
extraordinary.
In the wideness of the wilderness
God marked out a sanctuary—
a holy ground
on to which he invited me to stand:
bare sole against bare sand
so that my body should know in time
my soul's encounter with the eternal.
God sanctifying human time and space—
a bush—burning...
on such a small thing did the changing
of history depend.
A small thing
a strange thing—
and I could have walked by.
But I did not—
I took off my shoes and took the risk of
standing on that holy ground—
a mortal man, I dared to speak with the

© Olga Sapegina / Shutterstock.com

immortal and omnipotent God of my ancestors—
and my God transformed me.
History knows my name because God called it first.
An encounter—not in palace or temple—
not between God and the great and the good—
but an encounter next to a bush
between God and me—a man slow in speech—
unaware of my destiny...
An encounter such as can happen in this place—
where God enters the ordinary
to encounter his people—
coming into a place where many are gathered
in order to speak to sons and daughters
of his dreams for them:
to release them from that which holds them bound
to liberate them from their doubt and darkness
to send them renewed
restored
reinvigorated
forgiven
on the great adventure
of the journey to his Promised Land.

Reflection / symbolic gesture (creating holy ground)

'Bush' placed centrally (before liturgy)—with strips of flame-coloured cellophane in baskets close by—four (or more?)

Reconciliation stations set up beforehand but at this point priests are invited to come forward and take lit candles to where they will be sitting. As they go, the following prayer is said (perhaps several times—accompanying each priest...)

> May the blessing of God the Creator be upon this place...

May the blessing of God the Creator be upon this place
The blessing of Christ, Incarnate Redeemer—
The blessing of the Spirit, hallowing and healing—
The blessing of our Triune God on all who come in peace
and seek an encounter with the loving and divine.

As people celebrate the sacrament—or simply wish to acknowledge an encounter with God, they tie a strip of cellophane to the 'bush'. To add to the effect, the tree can be up-lit. Music and quiet songs are played at intervals.

Regathering

Simple reflection on what has happened—
the transformative encounter with God in the sacrament—
the importance of the prayer one for another—
and time to thank God and prepare to depart.

Reading

Exodus 3:13–15
The encounter with God ends when Moses is sent to the people to set them free...

Concluding Prayer

God of infinite power and tenderest mercy,
open our hearts and minds to awareness of your presence.
Challenge our complacency—
assure us of your forgiveness—
empower us to place before you
the sin which diminishes us as your children. Amen

Concluding Song

To celebrate the encounter with God.

WWW.WELLSPRINGS.ORG.UK/LITURGIES/RECONCILIATION_BURNINGBUSH.HTM

CAROL JERMAN

Carol's prayers

Choose one or two of the prayers that express what you think or use these prayers as ideas for your own.

Full of present moments

Thank you, Father, for your gift of today. It is full of present moments for your grace, full of more opportunities for your creative goodness than we can imagine. It is our time again to put our trust in you. Moment by moment, help us to live this day with a quiet mind, with a settled heart, at rest in you. Teach us again how to live in simple dependence upon you, as Jesus lived, with a heart open to receive the instruction of your Spirit. We give to you all our concerns, all the things that we will face today that seem too big for us. You are the Lord of all and therefore we commit this day to you, secure in the knowledge that your mercies, your loving-kindnesses, are new every morning. Amen

author

Carol Jerman is a retired teacher and has recently become a Reader in the Church in Wales. She takes people walking in the Berwyn mountains, accompanied by her llamas.

> Today, O Son of God and Son of man, is a time to know your power, so may we trust in your Lordship and see your saving grace

Grant to me this day...

Grant to me this day, Lord Jesus, that I may do no harm to anyone. You are kind to all that you have made, the God of justice and compassion. Help me simply to live in your goodness in all that I do and think and say. In Jesus' name, Amen

Help me today, dear Lord of all, in all the decisions that I must take. May your light shine again in my heart, showing me where I may be self-seeking, cowardly or manipulative. Help me to turn away from all these things, to be more like you, Lord Jesus. In your great mercy, Father, help me to live in humility and obedience, as a true disciple of Christ. In reverence for you, may I find wisdom. And what I ask for myself, I ask for the whole Church. In Jesus' name, Amen

Lord Jesus, what can I offer you today? What can I bring as worship? I would like to bring you an abundance of praise and thanksgiving, but I can find no praise in my heart, only brokenness and failure. I was following you, but I have come into wreckage, heartache and disappointment. It seems to be a long time ago that love for you, joy and faith rose like a flame from my heart. Now I am like a winter tree, ice-bound, as good as dead, without leaves, without fruit. But I trust in you, O my God, that you will send your springtime again into this soul that, in due season, life shall rise, and your own work will tell of your glory. Your faith doesn't fail, and darkness is the same as light to you. So I offer up my trust as praise. In the sorrow of my today, I confess that you are the faithful God, Lord Jesus Christ, my Saviour. Amen

Today, Lord Jesus, is a time for knowing you, so help us to live in your presence. Today, King and Saviour, is a time to hear your voice, so may we hear you speaking in our hearts. Today, O Son of God and Son of man, is a time to know your power, so may we trust in your Lordship and see your saving grace at work in our lives and in the lives of all around us, to the honour and glory of your name. Amen

Thank you, Lord, for the joy of being alive. Thank you for the beautiful world in which we live, for the love of family and friends and for good things without number to enjoy. Help us to value all your gifts today and to honour you in our enjoyment of them. As we enjoy them, help us to remember those for whom today is full of hardship, hunger, fear. Help us to know how best to give, how best to pray. May our lives express the love of Christ, today and every day. Amen

Today, Father, I can see your wisdom in leading me the way that I have come. I bow my knee in wonder at the way you turn everything to good. Yesterday's seeds, planted with tears, have become a harvest of joy. So help me again with your grace to plant seeds today that will grow into the blessings of tomorrow. In Jesus' name, Amen

Today, Lord Jesus, is a time for knowing you, so help us to live in your presence. Today, King and Saviour, is a time to hear your voice, so may we hear you speaking in our hearts

Give me the wisdom, Lord, not to waste today regretting the past or worrying about the future. Give me the grace to live in each moment with you, for now is the only time I have in which I can respond to the promptings of your Spirit. Help me not to waste today's opportunities to do good to others and to put my trust in you. Give me the courage to know that your grace is sufficient for everything that this day may bring. Amen

Give me the wisdom, Lord, not to waste today regretting the past or worrying about the future

Holy, holy, holy Lord, we lift our hearts in praise. We join in the song of all creation, telling of your goodness and your glory. While we have breath, we will praise your name. While it is today, we will tell your story. We will tell it to our children and to our children's children, so that they in their turn may tell it again, the story of the Father and the Son and the Spirit, the story of the Church and the song of the Lamb. May your name be praised, today and forever, our loving Creator, Father and Saviour. Amen

Speak to our hearts again, dear Lord, today, for in these moments of time, you can speak words that last forever, and draw from us responses of love and faith that can affect our lives for years to come. God of grace and love, do your will among us, in Jesus' name. Amen

Give us discernment, Father, to understand the challenges we face. Show us how to apply the wisdom of the past to the dilemmas of today. Guide us through all pitfalls and temptations. In the power of your Holy Spirit, may we find courage and compassion, so that we may be faithful and loving this day. Amen

Father, we offer to you our daily tasks, our work, as worship. Help us to do everything for your glory, so that when this day comes to an end, we may thank you for all your blessings. Amen

Speak to our hearts again

Prayer for stillness

God of stillness and
creative action,
help us to find space
for quietness today
that we may live
creatively,
discover the inner
meaning of silence,
and learn the
wisdom
that heals the world.
Send peace and joy
to each quiet place,
to all who are
waiting
and listening.
May your still small
voice be heard
through Christ, in
the love of the Spirit
Amen

God, of your goodness,
give me yourself,
for you are sufficient
for me.
I cannot properly ask
anything less, to be
worthy of you.
If I were to ask less
I should always
be in want.
In you alone,
do I have all.

JULIAN OF NORWICH

TONY HORSFALL

Tony's reflections

What do you see?

author

Tony Horsfall is a freelance trainer and retreat leader living in Yorkshire. He is the author of *Mentoring for Spiritual Growth* (2008) and *Working from a Place of Rest* (2010), both published by BRF.

Finding God in the present moment

Have you ever sensed God asking you to do something for which you felt inadequate? This was certainly Jeremiah's experience when he realised God was calling him to be a prophet. The story is recorded in Jeremiah 1. There the young 'prophet in the making' is reminded that God created him with this particular task in mind, and that he must not hide behind his youthfulness. God will accompany him, despite his fears, and the divine touch upon his mouth assures him that he will indeed

> Jeremiah had been given his first lesson in **receiving the word of the Lord**

speak the word of God.

At this point Jeremiah is asked a surprising question: 'What do you see, Jeremiah?' He answers with a statement of the obvious: 'I see the branch of an almond tree.' And then, making a play on words between the similar-sounding Hebrew words for 'watching' and 'almond tree', the Lord responds by saying, 'You have seen correctly, for I am watching to see that my word is fulfilled' (Jeremiah 1:11–12, NIV).

Without realising it, Jeremiah had been given his first lesson in receiving the word of the Lord, and it came about by simply noticing his surroundings. This discipline of awareness, the ability to 'see' what is around us, is a key aspect of the spiritual life. We are called to find God in the present moment, to become alive and alert to what he is doing in the here and now. If we have eyes to see, we can find God wherever we are and hear him speaking to us.

God is present to us in creation in two ways: firstly, through its grandeur and magnificence. For example, lofty mountain peaks, glorious sunsets, the wonder of a night sky, all speak eloquently of the greatness of God. Secondly, through the details of creation—God has written his word into the smallest fragments, and what we notice with our eyes can become for us parables of nature. If we have eyes to see and ears to hear, the word of the Lord will come to us through the world around us.

> Sometimes we are **wrapped up in our past**

The pace of modern life, however, can rob us of our ability to 'notice' God. We are too busy rushing from A to B to appreciate the beauty around us, let alone its detail. Furthermore, sometimes we are wrapped up in our past, caught up in regrets, robbed of our enjoyment of the present. Alternatively, we may be dreaming of the future, lost in thoughts about what may be, and blind to what is actually before us at this very moment. The poet W.H. Davies (1871–1940), in his poem 'Leisure', wistfully captures our dilemma: 'What is this life if, full of care, we have no time to stand and stare?'

Awareness Walk

One very simple way by which we can become more conscious of God's presence in the 'today' of our lives is through an *Awareness Walk*. It works likes this.

Go for a leisurely stroll, praying that God will guide your steps and asking that the Holy Spirit will make you alert to whatever he wants to bring to your attention. Then, walking slowly, notice what you notice.

Begin by experiencing the world around you through your five senses. Use each in turn to encounter a very real world. What do you see? What can you hear? Touch some things and feel their texture. What can you smell? Is there anything you can taste? Take in your surroundings, becoming aware of your environment, soaking up the moment.

Trust that in the process this is not by accident or chance but **something God planned**

As you do this, be aware of anything in particular that seems to grab your attention, that is interesting or curious, or towards which you feel drawn. Then take some time to ponder the significance of what you have noticed. How might it speak to you? In what way can this object or event be a parable to you, a sign or a symbol of spiritual truth? Trust that in the process this is not by accident or chance but something God planned.

As you return, take a moment to worship God and thank him for all he has made in its beauty and intricacy. Perhaps make a note in your journal of what you felt God was saying to you. Maybe share with a friend what has been important to you.

When we practise this simple exercise often, it becomes a way of seeing the world and of encountering God in the present moment. It becomes easier to recognise when God is drawing our attention to something significant, and our ears become more attuned to what he may be saying to us. We can do this wherever we are—in the countryside, but also in the city. It will help us to recognise the approach of God in other ways too—when we are watching a film, reading a book or doing our chores, for instance.

Traffic signs and speed bumps

I was staying at a hotel recently, and even though it was a dark, rainy November day, I went out for a breath of fresh air along the rather grand driveway. I had only just stepped out of the door when my attention was grabbed by a sign at the edge of the road, limiting cars to ten mph, and warning, 'Slow, speed bumps'.

Immediately a train of thought was triggered in my mind. How impossibly slow ten mph seems now, although to our grandparents it would have been daringly fast! And how essential the introduction of speed bumps has become in recent times. But most significantly, this thought: how necessary it is in modern life to tell people to slow down.

Then my thoughts turned towards my own hectic lifestyle with its inbuilt resistance to slowing down. Yet, isn't the sabbath commandment God's version of a stop sign? And shouldn't I thank God for the speed bumps he places in my own life that slow me down—the traffic delays, a dose of flu, an unexpected visitor, the gaps in my diary—rather than feel frustrated?

A simple walk became an avenue to communion with God for me, and this is what happens when we live in the present moment with spiritual awareness. What is it that you are seeing? And what is God saying?

A simple walk became an avenue to communion with God for me, and this is what happens when **we live in the present moment...**

A way of seeing the world

poem

Embracing God's World

These poems are taken from *Embracing God's World: prayers for the yearning heart*, BRF, 2007, a selection of prayers old and new made by Joyce Huggett. For further information, go to www.brfonline.org.uk.

author

Joyce Huggett is a well-known Christian author of bestselling books on listening to God. She is now based in the UK after years serving overseas.

Open to God

Prise open my fingers,
O God,
that nothing:
my cottage
my country
my culture
and no one:
my children
my companions
my confidantes
may keep me
from being radically open
to you
or prevent me from
saying yes to you.

JOYCE HUGGETT

A prayer of abandonment

Father, I abandon myself into your hands;
do with me what you will.
Whatever you may do, I accept all.
Let only your will be done in me,
and in all your creatures—
I wish no more than this, O Lord.
Into your hands I commend my soul;
I offer it to you with all the love of my heart,
for I love you, Lord, and so need to give myself,
to surrender myself into your hands without reserve,
and with boundless confidence,
for you are my Father.

CHARLES DE FOUCAULD (1858–1916)

Margaret's Space

Margaret Harvey is a retired priest in the Church in Wales. She has been running Coleg y Groes Retreat House. Margaret writes a regular column in *Quiet Spaces*.

It all depends on the tone of voice. Put an exclamation mark after it and click on the 'bold' icon and it becomes **'Today!'** barked out and demanding, about deadlines and pressure. Work has to be completed today. Results are expected today or as near today as possible. Today's news is on the TV or computer screen 'as it happens'. Thoughts, large or small, are passed on by text, email or mobile phone as soon as they come to mind. Experiences are shared immediately. Responses to disaster or tragedy, triumph and failure, political statements or anything else are sought as soon as a reporter with a microphone can be on the scene. 'Today' is the list of things I have to do or I haven't done. It is potentially full of tension and pressure. No wonder we have invented so many ways to escape from today. The escape may cause more problems than it solves; the misuse of alcohol or drugs are obvious examples. But most of us will have felt the need to escape from the realities or pressures of today. I guess that is part of what Jesus and friends were doing when they got into a boat to search out a quiet spot for recovery (see Heather Fenton's article on page 8). A whole travel industry taps into that longing to escape for a time.

Thoughts, large or small, are passed on by text, email or mobile phone **as soon as they come to mind**

Fantasy games and films offer another way to a different place and time. I'm writing this as *Avatar* has just arrived at local cinemas; an escape not just to a new planet but to a new body.

> We are called to live **in the moment** rather than for the moment...

Religion can be perceived as just another way of escape. We receive a variety of responses when we explain that we run a retreat house. 'How wonderful! That's just what I could do with. A chance to get away from the job/family/rat race...' Those 'down times' are really vital. Sometimes what's most important about a retreat can be allowing ourselves to stop, turning the phone off—it can take the whole week's retreat before it is possible to cope with switching off the mobile! But a retreat can also be an opportunity to discover resources to enable us to live in our today. In his famous classic *Self Abandonment to Divine Providence*, Jean Pierre de Caussade (1675–1751) uses the telling phrase 'the sacrament of the present moment'. We are probably used to the idea that a sacrament, a special event like baptism or the Eucharist, offers us the possibility of encounter with God. But de Caussade challenges us to discover each moment, our 'now', our 'today', as a gift of life too. We are called to live in the moment rather than for the moment. The section in the Sermon on the Mount that tackles anxiety (Matthew 6:25–34) tells us to 'consider'; to take time to notice the plants growing in the field or garden or roadside. We don't have to be on retreat to do this. We can build small pauses into the day; stop for a few seconds to look attentively at whatever is to hand, slow down when eating a quick snack in the middle of work or shopping and taste the food. I love the way Jesus gives people his full attention, being completely in the 'now' when, for example, he encounters a woman with a problem; he is attentive to her and it is the disciples who are in danger of missing the gift and the opportunity of the moment in their anxiety about pressures of time and social expectation (Luke 8:40–56).

As Tim Blewett reminds us (see pages 20–21), retreat houses can be busy places. I'm reminding myself to put into practice what I write!

LYNN CHAMBERS

Creative Ideas for Quiet Corners

This extract is taken from *Creative Ideas for Quiet Corners* by Lynn Chambers (Barnabas, 2008), a book that contains ideas for encouraging children and adults to find spaces for prayer.

author

Lynn Chambers is Priest-in-Charge of the Brechfa group of parishes in St David's Diocese in the Church in Wales.

Praying for others

This quiet corner gives us an opportunity to think about the people who are important in our lives. Taking time in choosing pebbles to represent people offers space to think about individuals. People are continually being changed by circumstances, relationships with other people and by their relationship with God. At first glance, one pebble may look like any other pebble but, like people, each pebble is individually formed. The shape and texture of a pebble are the result of continual washing by the sea, which shapes and smoothes them. The careful arrangement of pebbles on a mat gives us the opportunity to think about our relationships. A pebble placed at a distance from the others may represent someone living far away or it may represent someone living in the same house but seemingly remote.

The Bible focus encourages us to pray continually. The trust and peace associated with prayer are explored through images of water and reassuring words from the Bible. In the same way that the pebble has been shaped from a rough piece of stone through continual washing and smoothing, so our lives are shaped by our continued relationship with others and with God. Taking a pebble to represent all our prayers, and putting it in the pebble pool full of water, symbolises putting the people we love into God's hands and letting the Holy Spirit wash over them.

Getting started

Arrange some blue fabric on a table top to look like flowing water. Place a large bowl on the fabric on the table top. Ceramics or metal work well as there is a satisfying 'chink' when the pebble is placed in the water and makes contact with the bowl. However, for safety reasons, you may prefer to use a plastic

This quiet corner gives us an opportunity to **think about the people**

bowl. Glass, although attractive, is not suitable for young children.

Half fill the bowl with water. Lay a fabric table mat (or a piece of brown felt) in front of the bowl. Arrange pictures of rivers, waterfalls and seascapes on the blue fabric surrounding the bowl of water. Include pictures of the sea or rivers washing over pebbles.

Next to the pictures arrange cards showing the words from the 'Staying with the story' section. Place a basket of pebbles next to the table mat.

Stilling

Look at the pebbles in the basket and choose a pebble to represent you... Look at the colours in your pebble and feel the texture... When you are ready, place the pebble on the mat...

Think about the people in your family... Look at the pebbles in the basket again and choose some more pebbles to represent members of your family... Arrange the pebbles on the mat, some near your pebble and maybe some far away...

Think about your friends... Look at the pebbles in the basket again and choose some more pebbles to represent your friends... Place the pebbles on the mat...

Think about others who are important to you... maybe your teacher or your pet... Choose some more pebbles to represent them and place the pebbles on the mat...

Look at all the pebbles on the mat... Spend some time quietly talking to God about all the people that the pebbles represent...

God asks us to keep praying for others...

Bible focus

Never stop praying, especially for others. Always pray by the power of the Spirit. Stay alert and keep praying for God's people.
EPHESIANS 6:18 (CEV)

Staying with the story

God asks us to keep praying for others and he also asks us to trust him. Spend some time looking at the pictures of water as you read and think about the words on the cards. Use the following Bible verses: Jeremiah 17:7–8; Psalm 23:1–3; Psalm 17:6.

Gather all your pebbles together and put them back in the basket.

Choose one pebble to represent your prayers and hold it in your hand as you think about all the people who are important to you... Think about the pebble, the way it has been made, washed, shaped and smoothed by water... Think about God washing over and shaping the lives of the people you are praying for...

When you are ready, drop the pebble in the water and quietly thank God for listening and answering all your prayers.

Are there some other pebbles in the pool? Think about who put them there. You might not know who did it, but you can think about them all the same... Think about what situations and people the pebbles might represent... Pray for other people who have prayed at the pebble pool... You could use the following prayer.

Loving God, I bring to you all the people and situations that these pebbles represent. I pray also for all those who used these pebbles in their love and care for others. Amen

Living with the story

Make a pebble shape out of paper or card. You may like to write the words of Psalm 17:6 or Ephesians 6:18 on the pebble shape to remind you to pray. You may like to write the names of the important people in your life as a reminder to pray for them.

Prayer response

Lord Jesus, thank you for always being near to me. Please be near to all the people I love. Amen

Living the journey

Try one or more of the following activities.

- Keep a small pebble in your pocket or on your windowsill as a reminder to pray for others.
- Memorise the following words from Psalm 23:2–3 to remind you of God's love for you: 'You lead me to streams of peaceful water, and you refresh my life.'

Pilgrim's Progress

Three quarters of a million people in five years cannot be wrong! One website that gives the text of Bunyan's *A Pilgrim's Progress* claims that this number of people has accessed the text in that time. So who was Bunyan and what is his ongoing attraction?

...his vivid imagery

Born in Bedfordshire in 1628, John [Bunyan] came from a working-class family, his father earning a living as a tinker, mending kettles and pots

Born in Bedfordshire in 1628, John came from a working-class family, his father earning a living as a tinker, mending kettles and pots. He had very little schooling, having been educated at his father's house with other poor country boys. Like his father, he too became a tinker. At that time being a tinker was a lowly sort of occupation and had been associated with a nomadic lifestyle. He served in the parliamentary army between 1644 and 1647 as the civil war was nearing the end of the first stage. It is therefore obvious where he got some of his vivid imagery. In his autobiographical book, *Grace Abounding*, Bunyan describes

> **The Interpreter then called for a man-servant** of his, one Great-Heart, and bid him take a sword, and helmet, and shield; and, Take these my daughters, said he, conduct them to the house called Beautiful...

himself as having led an 'abandoned life' in his youth. Examples of sins to which he confesses are profanity, dancing and bell-ringing, probably all things he had in common with the people around him!

After his conversion, Bunyan became a popular preacher as well as a prolific author. In 1658, aged 30, he was arrested for preaching without a licence. Bunyan used his time in prison well, and is thought to have written *Pilgrim's Progress* in two parts, the first of which was published in London in 1678 and the second in 1684. As he was riding to London from Reading he caught a cold and developed a fever. He died at the house of his friend, John Strudwick, a grocer and chandler on Snow Hill in Holborn Bridge, on 31 August 1688. Here is an extract from his most famous work, *A Pilgrim's Progress*:

The Third Stage

The Interpreter then called for a man-servant of his, one Great-Heart, and bid him take a sword, and helmet, and shield; and, Take these my daughters, said he, conduct them to the house called Beautiful, at which place they will rest next. So he took his weapons, and went before them; and the Interpreter said, God speed. Those also that belonged to the family, sent them away with many a good wish. So they went on their way, and sang,

This place hath been our second stage:
Here we have heard, and seen
Those good things, that from age to age
To others hid have been.
The dunghill-raker, spider, hen,
The chicken, too, to me
Have taught a lesson: let me then
Conformed to it be.
The butcher, garden, and the field,
The robin and his bait,
Also the rotten tree, doth yield
Me argument of weight,
To move me for to watch and pray,
To strive to be sincere;
To take my cross up day by day,
And serve the Lord with fear.

Now I saw in my dream that they went on and Great-Heart before them. So they went, and came to the place where Christian's burden fell off his back and tumbled into a sepulchre. Here then they made a pause; and here also they blessed God. Now, said Christiana, it comes to my mind what was said to us at the gate, to wit, that we should have pardon by word and deed: by word, that is, by the promise; by deed, to wit, in the way it was obtained. What the promise is, of that I know something; but what is it to have pardon by deed, or in the way that it was obtained, Mr. Great-Heart, I suppose you know; wherefore, if you please, let us hear your discourse thereof.

The gospel of Christ as set out in the letter to the Romans is explained to Christina, after which the conversation continues thus:

Christiana: I thought so; for though my heart was lightsome and joyous before, yet it is ten times more lightsome and joyous now. And I am persuaded by what I have felt, though I have felt but little as yet, that if the most burdened man in the world was here, and did see and believe as I now do, it would make his heart the more merry and blithe.

The dialogue continues and the travellers move on together. Of course on their journey they meet many obstructions, including coming to the place where three rogues, Simple, Sloth and Presumption, had been.

Now I saw in my dream, that they went on until they were come to the place that Simple, and Sloth, and Presumption, lay and slept in when Christian went by on pilgrimage: and behold, they were hanged up in irons a little way off on the other side.

Mercy: Then said Mercy to him that was their guide and conductor, what are these three men; and for what are they hanged there?

Mr. Great-Heart: These three men were men of very bad qualities; they had no mind to be pilgrims themselves, and whomsoever they could, they hindered. They were sloth and folly themselves, and whomsoever they could persuade they made so too, and withal taught them to presume that they should do well at last. They were asleep when Christian went by; and now you go by, they are hanged.

Further, they would call the bread of God husks; the comforts of his children, fancies...

Mercy: But could they persuade any to be of their opinion?

Mr. Great-Heart: Yes, they turned several out of the way. There was Slow-pace that they persuaded to do as they. They also prevailed with one Short-wind, with one No-heart, with one Linger-after-Lust, and with one Sleepy-head, and with a young woman, her name was Dull, to turn out of the way and become as they. Besides, they brought up an ill report of your Lord, persuading others that he was a hard taskmaster. They also brought up an evil report of the good Land, saying, it was not half so good as some pretended it was. They also began to vilify his servants, and to count the best of them meddlesome, troublesome busybodies. Further, they would call the bread of God husks; the comforts of his children, fancies; the travel and labour of pilgrims, things to no purpose.

Christiana: Nay, said Christiana, if they were such, they shall never be bewailed by me: they have but what they deserve; and I think it is well that they stand so near the highway, that others may see and take warning.

WWW.CCEL.ORG/CCEL/BUNYAN/PILGRIM.V.V.HTML

My Reflections

© *Heather Fenton 2003*

This space is for you to make your own notes.

St Brendan and his companions set out one day on a pilgrimage into the unknown. This sculpture can be seen at Cahersiveen on the Ring of Kerry.

HEATHER FENTON

The prodigal decided today is better than tomorrow

As human beings we tend to put things off. 'Why do today what you can do tomorrow?' seems to be a good motto sometimes. Unfortunately, eventually some things become so urgent that we just have to do them, however uncomfortable that makes us feel. In the story of the prodigal son, we see the young lad going off full of confidence! He is going to start a new life without his father. He thinks he knows best. Time will tell. Keen to go, but not so keen to admit to the failure of his youthful dreams, he waits until the very last moment before deciding to go home and, by doing so, to admit to failure.

author

Heather Fenton works as a parish priest and an editor.

Sometimes we make big mistakes and then realise that we will have to revisit those mistakes. They begin by seeming far away but sooner or later return to stare us in the face, making emotional demands on us. So it was for the boy in the story. What started off as a grand adventure became a nightmare. He was sleeping in a pig-sty, and eating the pigs' food. I rather imagine him waking up one morning, cold, stiff and hungry, and realising that many of his father's hired men 'have food to spare, and I am starving to death' (Luke 15:17, NIV). In the end he had no real choice. Having made the decision to go back, he probably wondered what sort of response he would get. The consequences of yesterday are alive and kicking today, kicking him hard. He has no work, no money, nowhere to live. He has to acknowledge to himself that he is desperate.

The story of the prodigal son highlights how the events of a day can be good for some and apparently not so good for others. The father was delighted to have his son back. His response was one of joy, although I can't help feeling that it was also rather tactless. No gently bringing his other son round to the idea that his younger brother was home. Instead, party time! For the father, today was a good day.

Did he think his other son would be pleased? It does not come as any surprise to the reader that he became angry and refused even to go into the house. No,

Sometimes we make big mistakes and then realise that we will have to revisit those mistakes

the young lad's elder brother was far from delighted! It was a bad, a terrible day. He had always thought his father preferred his brother. Now he knew for sure. A day for stomping and for cursing and definitely not for celebrating! For the eldest son, it was not a good day.

And the lad himself? He was obviously very nervous. Was he going to be glad or sorry that he had resolved to do this today? Which of the alternative scenarios he anticipated when he woke up that morning turned out to be right? But he had made a bold decision. We could even say he made a good decision. He decided to go and attempt to sort it out. It could no longer wait!

Is God calling you to do anything about what lies in the past?
Is he calling you to do it today?

...it could no longer wait

What are we putting off? What needs to be done today? I once ended a sermon along the same lines with the words 'Do it now'. I was delighted when someone who had been in the congregation that day came up to me a few weeks later and said, 'I did what you said.' As I did not remember asking him to do anything (he was churchwarden at the time), I was a bit puzzled. So I asked him what he had done. The response was something like this: 'Well, I was dithering about buying a new car. After you said that, I went and did it, just like you said! It's sitting on my drive now.' My pleasure at discovering that he had paid attention was a bit short-lived, as that was not quite what I had meant!

Well, maybe that is what today has in store for you. Is God calling you to do anything about what lies in the past? Is he calling you to do it today? Are you the older brother, the father or the prodigal in the story? It can be found in Luke 15:11–32. There is much more to be unpacked in this story. But you could start today! Yes, that is this today. Not tomorrow. Today. Right now.

MAGGI DAWN

Giving it up

This extract is from the recently published book *Giving it up: Daily Bible readings from Ash Wednesday to Easter Day*, BRF, 2009. For further information, go to www.brfonline.org.uk.

Lost and found: two lost sons

Then Jesus said, 'There was a man who had two sons. The younger of them said to his father, "Father, give me the share of the property that will belong to me." So he divided his property between them. A few days later the younger son gathered all he had and travelled to a distant country, and there he squandered his property… A severe famine took place throughout that country, and he began to be in need. So he went and hired himself out to one of the citizens of that country, who sent him to his fields to feed the pigs. He would gladly have filled himself with the pods that the pigs were eating; and no one gave him anything. But when he came to himself he said, "How many of my father's hired hands have bread enough and to spare, but here I am dying of hunger! I will get up and go to my father, and I will say to him, 'Father, I have sinned against heaven and before you; I am no longer worthy to be called your son; treat me like one of your hired hands.'" So he set off and went to his father. But while he was

author

Maggi Dawn is an Anglican minister, currently serving as Chaplain to Robinson College, Cambridge University. She has written Bible reading notes and books and is also author of a number of worship songs and hymns.

still far off, his father saw him and was filled with compassion; he ran and put his arms around him and kissed him. Then the son said to him, "Father, I have sinned against heaven and before you; I am no longer worthy to be called your son." But the father said to his slaves, "Quickly, bring out a robe—the best one—and put it on him; put a ring on his finger and sandals on his feet. And get the fatted calf and kill it, and let us eat and celebrate; for this son of mine was dead and is alive again; he was lost and is found!" And they began to celebrate.

> It was also unfair on the older brother...

'Now his elder son was in the field... He called one of the slaves and asked what was going on. He replied, "Your brother has come, and your father has killed the fatted calf..." Then he became angry and refused to go in. His father came out and began to plead with him. But he answered his father, "Listen! For all these years I have been working like a slave for you... yet you have never given me even a young goat so that I might celebrate with my friends. But when this son of yours came back, who has devoured your property with prostitutes, you killed the fatted calf for him!" Then the father said to him, "Son, you are always with me, and all that is mine is yours. But we had to celebrate and rejoice, because this brother of yours was dead and has come to life; he was lost and has been found."'

LUKE 15:11–32 (ABRIDGED)

The third lost-and-found story in Luke's Gospel is the prodigal son. To be prodigal means to be generous to the point of being a reckless spendthrift, to give without concern for whether the gift will be wasted. It's a term that obviously fits the younger son well. All his actions from the very beginning of the story are outrageous. Within his culture, to ask for his inheritance early was tantamount to wishing his father was already dead. It was also unfair on the older brother, for, by dividing the family fortune in two, the younger brother simply walked away with his share in realised assets, leaving his father and brother to manage a vastly reduced estate. To make matters worse, having taken all that money out of the

The younger son gathered all he had and travelled to a distant country

estate, he squandered it. Eventually he found himself flat broke, discovered that his friends were only fair-weather friends, and had to take the lowliest of jobs, keeping pigs. He was so hungry that he would gladly have eaten the pigs' food—something especially repugnant for a Jew—but he was denied even this, which sent the clear message that he was of less value than a pig.

The bad behaviour and shocking

...sent the clear message that he was of **less value than a pig** wastefulness of the son are beyond doubt, but I think there's a bit of a twist in the tale. I notice that the son wastes his money by spending it all not just on himself but on his wayward friends. Have you ever stopped to wonder where he learned to be quite so outrageously, unquestioningly open-handed? You could argue that his father should have been sterner, more intent on teaching his young son self-discipline; that instead of parting so easily with the inheritance, he should have pulled his son into line. But the father himself is outrageously generous and is far more interested in building a relationship with his two sons than looking after the family wealth. Dividing the property for his son was, in itself, lavish to the point of recklessness, carried out in the full knowledge that the resources would probably be wasted. Yet it seems that he would rather see his money trickling down through the cracks than risk such anger and resentment brewing in his son that he would lose him for ever.

So overflowing with love for him that he could not bear to be without him

When the son, without a second thought, is over-generous towards his profligate friends, I can't help thinking that he's a chip off the old block. He has learnt that money is important only insofar as it supports friendship, kinship and love. Where did he learn that lesson? From his prodigal father, perhaps?

When the son finally heads home, his father is not only waiting for him but actually runs out to meet him. In that culture, dignified men did not run to meet their guests, but this father ran to his son, so overflowing with love for him that he could not bear to be without him. Danish theologian Søren Kierkegaard pointed out that what connects the three lost-and-found stories is this action of going out to look. The woman doesn't just wait for the coin to reappear but turns the house upside down until she finds it, the shepherd leaves the 99 to go and find the one, and the father doesn't wait for his son to come home but goes out to find him. We don't have to come knocking on heaven's door after all: long before heaven comes into view, God is already halfway down the road to show us in.

What's interesting, though, is that the father goes out looking in this way not just once but twice, for there are two lost sons in this story. The older son never left home but he's lost in such a sea of resentment that, when the party begins, he stays outside, sulking. He has good reason to feel put upon, of course. His younger brother, having wasted his own half of the inheritance, is now enjoying a huge, expensive feast which is being paid for out of the elder brother's share of the estate. His prodigal father is (dare we think it?) even worse than his younger brother. He's wasteful, excessive in his generosity.

The character of the older brother seems to be a direct reply to the Pharisees and scribes, in response to whose criticism Jesus told the three lost-and-found stories. The older brother is the upstanding but critical Pharisee who not only knew the religious rules but actually kept them all. In our context, the older brother is the upright, devoutly religious person, the respected yet resentful churchgoer. He is the ultimate insider, someone who controls the committee meetings, holds the keys, keeps the books, reads the lessons, leads the intercessions. But in the story it turns out that he is not inside at all, but outside, because even though we may live on the property, a cold heart removes us from God's presence into a darkness of our own making. No matter how perfectly we keep our religion, it's our heart that places us inside or outside God's presence.

The father is no more fazed by his over-responsible, self-righteous son than he is by the repentant good-time boy. Out goes the father once again, not satisfied until all his children are by his side, not merely sharing an inheritance but rejoicing in being together. Prodigal son—or prodigal father? Two lost sons—or one searching father? In the end, the story isn't so much about one lost son or two but about the unstinting generosity of God, whose love casts reason, convention and dignity aside.

Long before heaven comes into view, God is already halfway down the road to show us in

MARTYN PAYNE

Psalm 6

tears in the night

author

Martyn Payne is a member of the Barnabas children's ministry team and runs events for children and training events for teachers. He has wide experience of working with schools and churches to explore ways of opening up the Bible with children and is the author of several books. This idea is taken from the website www.barnabasinchurches.org.uk, where you can find many more ideas that can be used with children, all free of charge.

On your marks:

The Psalms are an amazing collection of poems, prayers and songs of praise and have been the staple diet of worship for Jews as well as Christians for centuries. They give us words for all sorts of occasions and moods as we work out our faith in God in the rough and tumble of everyday life. Many children will never have come across this book and may be surprised to discover that, for example, as well as expressing thanks and delight in God, it is also OK to argue with God, express despair and depression, shout angrily about things that are wrong and even have doubts about God's love. All this is in the Psalms and a lot more. It is an important resource to help our children grow into a mature faith.

They give us words for all sorts of occasions and moods as we work out our **faith in God**

Get set:

Read through the psalm first before you work with your group. Look at different translations. The verses quoted in the outline below are from the CEV (Contemporary English Version). Any specific materials needed to step into this particular psalm are included in the instructions below. The outline includes: a key verse; a brief introduction; an idea for acting out the psalm; prompts to talk about the psalm; a craft idea; some new ways to retell the psalm; a suggestion for reflection on the psalm; and finally a focus for praying for others with this psalm.

Go!

Key verse: *'My groaning has worn me out. At night my bed and pillow are soaked with tears' (v. 6).*

This isn't so much a psalm as a loud sob! It is a prayer that is soaked in tears and the writer—quite possibly David—is crying his heart out (vv. 6–8).

It is interesting to speculate what it was in David's life that caused so much distress. Perhaps it comes from the time when he was scared to death by Saul, who had hurled spears at him to kill him (1 Samuel 18:10–11); or maybe it was when he heard that the priest Ahimelech and his sons had been murdered by Saul, just because they had shown hospitality to David (1 Samuel 22)? 'Hateful people' (Psalm 6:8) have been responsible for assassination attempts and the death of the innocent—no

> The Psalms are an amazing collection of poems, prayers and songs of praise...

wonder he is scared and in tears he calls out to God.

Whatever the occasion for the outburst, it has become a psalm that has given many down the ages words to talk to God when everything seems hopeless and unutterably sad. It is a psalm for those worn out by life's cruel twists, red-eyed with grief, sleepless with worry and troubled by fears. This really is a prayer from the heart.

Words to talk to God...

It is a psalm for those worn out by life's cruel twists, red-eyed with grief, sleepless with worry and troubled by fears

Act out the Psalm

Take some time to explore the feelings in this psalm by inviting everyone to become statues of the various emotions that the writer shares with us. It might help to stand everyone in a circle facing outwards and give them time to think of a suitable pose, until a leader calls '3, 2, 1, turn' and all face inwards to show their chosen interpretation of the following aspects of the psalm:

- Fear
- Exhaustion
- Restlessness
- Despair
- In tears
- Anger
- Hope

As with many of the psalms, the writer speaks not just to God but also to him- or herself. One of the ways God answers our prayers is by giving us the words to speak out to ourselves, to assure us that God hears and will help.

Work out as a group in what direction they will face and what body shape they might adopt for someone praying to God and then talking to themselves—perhaps looking upward and outward at first (vv. 1–5) and then with a more introverted pose second (vv. 6–10).

Now put the statue ideas and the 'direction' for each half of the psalm together. Imagine it is a silent movie made up of a series of frames interspersed by captions with the psalm's words, section by section. Perhaps you could write out the verses as large captions. Finally add in some appropriate music. Take some digital pictures to record the result.

Talk through the Psalm

No one gets through this life 'tear-free' and Christians can find themselves in places of deep despair just like anyone else. Jesus tells us that 'while you are in the world, you will have to suffer' (John 16:33); the difference will be that Jesus promises to be there with us and has guaranteed a way through it all in the end.

Has anyone ever been so upset that they couldn't sleep?

Has anyone ever experienced this level of sadness? (Take care not to force anyone to share here, if they don't want to.)

Is it really possible to pray in such a state?

How can we help each other when we get this low?

How can we develop an instinct to pray whatever the circumstances?

One secret to prayer in such situations is that the person praying is honest about how he or she is feeling and acknowledges this (as in v. 1). The writer here says that his/her real fear is that all this has happened as a punishment for something he/she has done wrong. This

> No one gets through this life **'tear-free'**

is a very common response when 'bad stuff' happens to us and of course it is not necessarily the case.

The psalmist is also honest about his impatience with God (v. 3). Why aren't there any instant answers? And what's the point of all this being 'the death of him'? How does that help (vv. 4–5)?

Are we honest in our praying?

How would you respond to someone talking to you and praying like this?

And finally there is also honesty about wanting 'to get his own back' (v. 10). Getting even is a very human instinct; not to acknowledge that can be hypocritical and maybe dangerous.

Do we bring a pretend 'Christian' self to God in prayer or is it the real me?

Getting even is a very human instinct

Craft the Psalm

The key phrases of honest grief in this psalm are:

My bones tremble; I am in deep distress; my feeble body; my groaning has worn me out; sorrow has made my eyes dim; my sight has failed.

The key pleas and questions from the psalm are:

Have pity; heal me; don't punish me; come to my rescue; leave me alone; how long will it be?

Using teardrop shapes for the first set of words and speech-bubble shapes for the second, create a shaped poem of the psalm, arranging the teardrops and speech bubbles to make a further appropriate shape or shapes, such as a key word, an exclamation mark or the outline of a pillow.

You could work on this individually or as a group to make an illustrated version for the psalm.

Retell the Psalm

Use the tune and words of the song 'Kum Ba Yah' with a younger group, adding in some additional verses such as:

Someone's scared, Lord
Someone's tired, Lord
Someone's troubled, Lord
Someone's sleepless, Lord
Someone's hurting, Lord

With an older or mixed age group, use this version as an inspiration:

Is it my fault, God?
Do I deserve such grief?
I'm shattered, Lord.
It's beyond belief!

I'm distraught, disturbed
Despairing and drained
I need you, Lord

—I can't be blamed.

I want my life now,
Not at some future date.
I'll be dead before you answer
If it goes on at this rate!

I'm crying my eyes out
I've a tear-soaked pillow
I can hardly see out
And my eyes hurt me so.

It's all their fault
They did it to me
Oh help me please, God.
Oh set me free!

Reflect on the Psalm

As you read the psalm slowly verse by verse, put down carefully and thoughtfully the following objects (3-D models or pictures), using a base cloth, which is in the shape of an instrument (perhaps a harp), as for all these reflections on the psalms.

- ❖ A figure kneeling (v. 1)
- ❖ A figure stretched out flat on the ground exhausted (v. 2)
- ❖ A clock or watch (v. 3)
- ❖ A cross (vv. 4–5)
- ❖ A small handkerchief and small (doll's house) pillow or cushion (vv. 6–7)
- ❖ An open hand and ear (vv. 8–9)
- ❖ A fist (v. 10)

Pause and then ask some open-ended questions:

I wonder which part of this psalm you like the best?

I wonder if there is a part of it you don't like?

I wonder which part is especially for you at the moment?

I wonder...

> Do we bring a pretend 'Christian' self to God in prayer or **is it the real me?**

Finish by reading Psalm 56:8, which could so easily relate directly to Psalm 6 and assures us of what is written in verses 8a–9 of Psalm 6.

Pray for others with this psalm

Pray for all those who are sick and suffer sleepless nights.

Quiet Spaces subscriptions

Quiet Spaces is published three times a year, in May, September and January. To take out a subscription, please complete this form, indicating the month in which you would like your subscription to begin.

❑ I would like to take out a subscription myself

Name ______________________________

Address ______________________________

Postcode ____________ Telephone Number ______________________________

Email ______________________________

❑ Please do not send me further information about BRF publications.

❑ I would like to give a gift subscription (please complete your name and address above and details of the person you want to give a subscription to below)

Gift subscription name ______________________________

Gift subscription address ______________________________

____

______________________________ Postcode ____________

Please send beginning with the Jan 11 / May 11 / Sep 11 issue: (delete as applicable)

(please tick box)	UK	SURFACE	AIR MAIL
Quiet Spaces	❑ £16.95	❑ £18.45	❑ £20.85

Please complete the payment details below and send this coupon, with payment to: BRF, 15 The Chambers, Vineyard, Abingdon OX14 3FE.

Method: ❑ Cheque (payable to BRF) ❑ Mastercard ❑ Visa ❑ Maestro

Card no. ❑❑❑❑❑❑❑❑❑❑❑❑❑❑❑❑❑❑

Valid from ❑❑❑❑ Expires ❑❑❑❑ Issue no. of Maestro card ❑❑❑

Security Code ❑❑❑

Signature ______________________________ Date ____/____/____

All orders must be accompanied by the appropriate payment.

BRF is a Registered Charity

PROMO REF: QSTODAY

To order *Quiet Spaces* or other BRF publications mentioned in this journal, visit your local Christian bookshop or go to BRF's website www.brfonline.org.uk.